Where *Here* Is Hard to Say

Where *Here* Is Hard to Say

POEMS

Gordon Johnston

MERCER UNIVERSITY PRESS | MACON, GEORGIA
2023

MUP/ P680/908-0

© 2023 by Mercer University Press
Published by Mercer University Press
1501 Mercer University Drive
Macon, Georgia 31207
All rights reserved

27 26 25 24 23   5 4 3 2 1

Books published by Mercer University Press are printed on acid-free paper that
meets the requirements of the American National Standard for Information
Sciences—Permanence of Paper for Printed Library Materials.

Printed and bound in the United States.

This book is set in Adobe Caslon Pro and Georgia (display).

Cover/jacket design by Burt&Burt.

ISBN   978-0-88146-908-0
Cataloging-in-Publication Data is available from the Library of Congress

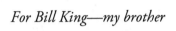

For Bill King—my brother

Acknowledgments

These poems appeared in the chapbook *Durable Goods* (Finishing Line Press, 2021):
"Cheat River: Packing the Pack"; "High Falls, Shaver's Fork of the Cheat"; "Photograph, 1941"; "*Bi-*"; "Even the Dirt"; "After Tom's Father Died"; "His Empty Oil Tin"; "Note at the Trailhead"; "Letter to My Brother from Seven Islands Shoals"

"Border Waters" appeared in *Susurrus*

"His Empty Oil Tin" and "Estuary" also appeared in *Southern Poetry Review*

While writing the poems in this collection, I received generous moral, spiritual, and material support from more sources than I can name; I am abidingly grateful to that community. I offer special thanks to my partner and co-pilgrim Pamela and to Emma, Micah, and Graham Johnston for their intrepid, hilarious spirits, for humoring my need for river, swamp, and trail time, and for being the first friends of my writing. These poems took on greater grace and clarity thanks to the suggestions of Bill King and Anya Krugovoy Silver. R.E.M., Folk Implosion, the Wood Brothers, Mavis Staples, and Wilco helped me keep the faith—as did studio talk with artists Eric O'Dell, whose painting graces the book cover, and Sherrie Jamison. Roger Jamison and the community of potters around his anagama kiln in Juliette, Georgia gave me sweat equity in a craft less solitary than poetry. Matt Harper wrote with me regularly and floated parts of the Flint, Etowah, Suwannee, and Ocmulgee with me. I'm grateful to Bill King for being my guide to Shaver's Fork of the Cheat, Blackwater Canyon, and the Dolly Sods Wilderness. Marc Jolley and Marsha Luttrell at Mercer University Press have (almost) infinite patience. I'm also thankful to the College of Liberal Arts and Sciences at Mercer University for the sabbatical that let me complete the collection; Deneen Senasi's Faculty Research and Writing Colloquium and

Griffith funds for travel from Mercer's English Department were especially helpful. A writing residency at the Lillian Smith Center was also a godsend.

Contents

I. Horizon Lines

II. Lonely Middles

III. LEAVING NO TRACE

IV. Whether to Make Yourself

Even if the world was perfect it wouldn't be.
　　　　　—Yogi Berra

Humbly accept the word planted in you, which can save you.
　　　　　—James 2:3

I. Horizon Lines

The deep surrounded me.
                    —Jonah 2:3

Where *Here* is Hard to Say

Floating the Ocmulgee on a September morning,
launching from one ruined ferry to land at another,
passing under busy bridges as if between the legs of altars,
this canoe is merely part of the pour: a shape the river pushes,
with no place to put her, with no plan other than
gravity, and an obsessive will. A soul in the boat
becomes a pulse through the sunlit synapses of an aquifer,
the maze of sandstone with its one way through, that
only gap. Sun dapples on ripples and on
sycamore leaves that almost stroke the flow the canoe
cruises. The gar still in the skin of the surface as a slim
metal needle drawn to a pole truer than north—the buzzard
whose glide circles slowly upstream—there's no
pinning them to a static map. The rivershed humps and rucks, not
a rod of it is flat. Its lives conflue, with an each-ness in a motion
that all that floats, sinks, suspends, weathers, or dissolves
joins and drives. To be present in this place of no place,
is to always both leave and arrive, to float, to see, to go—
to ride the one grace for all that has ever been alive.

Trash Fish

People pack pistols to blow holes in the big ones—
carp and alligator gar and redhorse. As a kid
of Zebcos and bobbers, I found them dead, wide-eyed
on Brier Creek's banks, flies rising from wounds the size
of my fist. At first their bodies seemed to me to provoke
buckshot: the gar-snout toothed like a saw, baracudic,
the carp and redhorse heavy, scaled like dragons, aloof,
but the more I found, looking at each a long time as a kid does
at a corpse when no adult is around, the greater my sympathy
grew—how awful for a fish, to die on the ground, outside
the element that had always floated you. The day I saw
a 'gator gar nosing along the still gold skin of a July cove, looming
like a zeppelin through the amber stew at the edge of air,
I stared three minutes after it was gone. An old woman told me
gar have a lung for when they can't gill enough oxygen.
They grunt with it. *Them gar and carp, they grow to kingdom come,*
she said, *long as you, if they's let be.* I imagined a fish,
five feet long, needle-toothed, cruising toward knee-deep me:
the strange anger that made fishermen bludgeon them
and fire sawed-off .410s at their silhouettes in the shallows
almost made sense. Twenty years on rivers later, I've never
seen a dirt fish half that size. It's not fear. We hate what we can't eat—
covet every breath and growth we can't have.
Creatures so much older than us, so much more certain to survive,
we can't stand to leave alive.

A Few Confluences in Blackwater Canyon

The first one that occurs to me is underfoot—
the path down from the rim that splits into strands
    which braid back together, a flow that keeps
dividing around washed-out root-nets of spruce,
    steep granite outcrops, hells of rhododendron,
and mudholes. Always the ways re-meet: one flow
    that wants to go to where the river creases
the canyon, rock bottom. You're smacked around
    by the gorge's downhill willfulness. You get to
meet the wild main channel and maybe catch
    a tiger trout only if you're willing to double
back often, to go slow in slick places and fall where you
    have to. The slippery trip turns you into a trickle,
sends you sideways to wind downward, drips you ledge
    to ledge until, stretched thin from reaching your left
boot to a grounded root and gripping a sapling to stop
    your slide, you come to the white gout of current
that accepts every other body into its own, that same old change.
    A river has always just arrived and just gone.
That's confluence number two: past and present un-fork
    into future as you watch the pour through a chute,
see the foam churned in a corner-eddy of the receptive, placating
    pool. The way the plunging river gulps air and whips up
a rotating, tea-edged meringue—this conflues silt, spruce-root,
    and vintage rain in a sweet, sugarless froth, the canyon's
only softness save moss. The bus-sized boulders lean, mum,
    as you try high and low for a path over or between,
thanking your god for a body that winds and bends, that
    leaps and can roll if the stone it lands on slants or wobbles.
Re-meet the self of meat, bone, and muscle in these gymnastics
    and the supple, strike-and-bolt strength of a fish half brook trout,
half brown, cold lightning to which the river is ground.

All morning, these meetings, these splittings and bindings.
I'm eddied upstream by the thunder of the falls whalloping 'round its prow
of rock until I'm landed, misted, not dissolving, on a wet slab
where the river's tonnage, falling, particle-izes, pools, then rolls on, whole.
Stranger here, I press my palms to my ears—hear my pouring
heart and the Blackwater's shatter as one, as if they've never been apart.

Tyger Trout

The third cast after my half-climb, half-fall
down the canyon's steep west wall, his lightning strike
    comes. Pretty much any trout sets off a charge in me,
but when my rod lifts these strong fish just free
    of the current, not yet landed—when I can
see them whole and writhing, cold and bright—
    it's like a nurse yells *Clear!,* all hands let go,
and I'm electrocuted back to life.
    Beauty cracks like that. Can arc through you to live-wire
two bodies together between cataract and bedrock.
    This wet tiger, alive mid-air between mountains,
thrashing, mazey-moled, a brainy explosive, shorts out
    every other mortal glory. His fluid, furious elegance,
as long as my forearm and stronger, hid, somehow,
    in six inches of transparent flow. Seeing the white-edged fins,
the perfect animal proportions—the power catches and releases me.
    Here's the hook I can't throw: tiger trout are human-made.
Brookie milt sowed over the roe of browns in a distant tank
    fired this vermiculated, clear-jade torpedo.
Some grunt toted dozens of him in buckets from truck to river—
    with grubby mitts poured them in. They're sterile. Can't repeat
themselves. I feel chest pain knowing it. Also a strange shame.
    I reel. I grasp his firm slime. Kiss it. We both quiver
in the grip of wild systole, caught and freed. Not tame.

Heard of Turtles

They burrow into the bottom, come winter,
gilling oxygen from the silty flow—
their anal outlet reverses to an in-go.

Each becomes a Kevlar holster for a heart
that slows from twenty-five rounds
a minute, full auto, to one, to save ammo.

Chilled, their small pumps keep the crawl of blood
mapping their veins glacially slow. Even sub-zero,
sunk like stones in the river's frozen holes, they grow.

Spring: once the pines' saffron pollen has sifted all,
then sunk in rinses of rain or dew, they un-die—
back out of mud and weakly rise. To summit

a rotting stump takes a tremulous, agonized hour,
but once there, a pot on a sun-stoked stove,
a red-ear's blood gradually comes to simmer.

Through the pieced-together crock of shell, heat
ripples, licking along the backbone like a slow fuse.
Each cooter's clay is fired from the outside in

in the kiln of noon. What must that be like, light
quickening your eye, launching you in the face
of threat into a fast dive—or, on land, draw-

bridging yourself inside? No wonder they wart
warm river rocks in mudpie choirs, mutely singing
as they stoke their green-gold, underwater fires.

Will

In March and April only, when the crappie swam shallow
to spawn, my father quit digging worms and bought bait—
minnows, from a dank shop where a leathery owner
would dip from a bubbling cement tank
and pour into our bucket a living silver tongue
of shiners, two dollars a dozen.
They hung in their squat silo of water, plural, one-willed,
fins idling, flickering like a volley of arrows impossibly paused.
I learned not to grab—to hang my open hand among them,
let them calm, then to finger-pin one, a shivering sliver
of muscle, against my palm. To my dad, a speckled perch
was worth ten of these fry. To me, ten hooked specks
didn't buck and writhe not to die half as hard as one shiner did.
A grown-up minnow would be one fierce fish, I said.
When we got home at sunset, he replied *We'll see*,
then freed the last four three-inchers into our rain barrel.
Typical boy, I forgot—went on to other lore.
Two winters froze and thawed the drum, made it seep.
Come May, the barrel seeming empty, I leaned and looked:
in the bottom, water one hand deep, a knife-fight—
two ten-inch blades slashing for their dim, narrow life.

Letter to Meriwether Lewis from Big Bend Dam

Debths was your word for the deep reaches
of the Missouri River, casting a (mis)spell on me
      that grants the great surging height and weight
of water the power to bankrupt the Great Plains—
      your spirit, too. Rods and surveyor's chains
and steam, the best steel would come to nothing against
      the megatonnage of this massive drainage,
this river that held nothing back—poured the whole
      winter snowpack into bulldozing its own banks.
You saw groves of trees, high hills, acres of loam blown,
      as if the will of the half-million-mile watershed were
to spend its infinity of plenty in a single spring. I'm glad
      you can't see it now, laked, lapping fatly, licking the concrete.
Your corps of souls, poling against the current, shrunk to a string
      of frog eggs, slopping on the chop and glut, daily needed
soundings to believe in a bottom, a fundament under the epic pour.
      You banked data in self-defense against the Missouri
and Columbia, their continental, tectonic continuum—nations
      human, animal, arboreal, every life between oceans
tributary to them. The way grasslands, Rockies, and redwoods owed
      the rivers all gathers in your one-syllable, cosmic typo
—*depth* and *debt* (even *death*)—coins that not a drop, rock, or noggin
      of wet silt could ever be owned.
The vast lake, blue-green, ripples in its sleep.
      Its depth and every mile of its shoreline known.
Two waves break, so far apart each seems alone.

Kayak at Bat Hour

Even at my feet on my porch at midnight, she begs
   to be on moving water—to take her place in a current
that would carry us, goad her nose through shallows
   into active eddies below falls where she could chase her tail.
Even on this concrete she seems to float, her belly so minimally
   grazing the ground that she seems to sit up, ears pricked,
fixed by a sense I lack on a life wild, lean, and well-fed
   that she aches to hunt down. Its rank scent calls her to leave
even such a smitten friend as me. In her muscle-swells
   at shoulder and haunch, her snout and tail on point, I see
her breath held: she would drag me in this dark down a creek
   gouged in the devil woods to a frothing, moon-fey shoal, arching
its grizzled back against us, hissing through its bared teeth
   in the half-light. She would plunge me with joy into the fight,
her love of me made complete in the eager forfeit of our one life.

Bond Swamp Bottomland

The swamp, like a pitcher plant or spider web, accepts
all comers. She let me into her cane brake's maze, that green
dream of raw spears, flutes, and fishing poles, then kept me,
    tangled, a years-long day. I lost, found, despaired of the way.
Rivercane sifted me. Thicket and brier scratched me, bled me
clean, catching me like a nit in her comb. She flicked me out,
    finally, onto a stream-bend beach of stones, set just so,
between undercut banks of meat-red clay. She emptied me
like a coil-built bowl, blew the thistle-fletched dart of me
    out her reed barrel. I lay down to be drowned or not in the warble
of water, saw one wall of the creek-cut offering coontie root,
the other, white clay. Springwater filled my ears, told me the way
    to the river. Creek-talk stood me up straight, as awake as yaupon,
as aimed as a tempered arrow drawn on an osage orange bow.
Notched on one string in a web of many, I still wait to be let go.

Birches

They grow by gradually skinning themselves,
baring their inner layer to the thin air and the weather,
their peels like old prayer flags, shouted down to shreds
by the gales in Tibetan passes—though the birches unreel
their outer selves slower than the written-on cloth
unravels. These trees' nature is to shed. In this stand of them,
a wish to stay in their shade comes, a yen to circle each trunk,
feel the bark crack, frizz, and uncurl for a moon or two.
You think *I will loop and loop the grove in its slow whirl,*
see each tree unscroll—but in a quarter hour you're too cold.
(Always, through mountain birches, a wind sows.) Even as
you go, buoyed by the sphagnum of shed bark, the trunks sort
and sift you through the perfect accident of their order—
their limber girth, their careful posture. Several felled by wind,
grown too close to their kin to fall, are straight even as they lean.
Their dropped branches moss-over in hummocks, gray as sea swells—
springy, mortal, fey. They have such gentle give that you will
still dream of lying down there, long after you've gone away.

On Screamer Mountain, Shelf Lichen

seems self-liking, because, while beauty is in the eye of the beholder,
strength is in the inverted L of this upholder – fungus that keeps
   its thallus-shoulders straight. In a meringue of wood rot, pride
of posture startles and inspires. The colony's comportment –
   a propriety as light and chaste as chipped bone china,
with the patina of a sweet great aunt's last RSVP to tea.
   They grow in a staggered order, as if on risers, row
on row, their pleated underparts like the crinolines
   of a choir poised to sing as soon as a conductor
comes. Until then, each brings rectitude to her
   sprawled, ruined tree. Honors oak's memory.
Collectively discreet, they politely digest
   the dead, gracing snags with ivory lace
ledges that are like the last frayed pages
   of a long fable, waiting to be read
to a girl already sleepy, already
   tucked in bed.

Border Waters

Most of my life I've bridged them—
let the rise of concrete, steel, or wood in the road

carry me over to the other county, state, or country
which I've shot through, bullet piercing a paper target.

There was pleasure in passing over a line,
making progress toward a place I needed to be

with minimal resistance from the miles between.
How much of being human is making up lines,

setting edges and borders just so you can cross them?
I'm still a fired slug, but losses have slowed me some.

Now I look when I come to crossings, upstream and down,
knowing the border the dead penciled there, but seeing

the real river, too—never still, where folks fish and drown.
Welcome to South Carolina, a road sign on the Savannah says.

Seeing it as a boy, I felt far gone from home: out of bounds.
I mistook an imaginary line set by some king for the reason

the river was there—believed that under the water the map's
black ink was etched in the karst and fossil coral and sands milled

from stone over a billion years, as if watersheds, like kid-me,
were obedient. One good flood, one broken bridge, one trip

on foot or horseback, one paddled boat and up we grow.
Every straightness and solidity blurs and melts as the river goes

easily where it wants to go—a current of rock, forest, storm,
and earth that shifts but never slows, that breaks its own banks,

dissolving and carrying everything, me included, in its motion.
Welcome, South Carolina, to being a single salt-grain in the ocean.

II. Lonely Middles

Let me show you where I live among my people.
—Revelation 21:2

Photograph, 1941

My father's father, younger than I am,
      squats in his black suit, his arm around
his five-year-old son, whose own arm
      drapes over his dad's shoulder. Behind them,
the apple tree that persisted until I came,
      behind it the board fence of their big yard
that was the very small Johnston farm,
      where corn, tomatoes, potatoes, greens,
turnips, pecans, pears, and a milk cow prospered.

      The black and white photo seems too bright.
The decades have blurred their smiles and lightened
      edges in the print. The intensity of the morning
sun is not what makes the image sing. The boy and man
      cast a dark shadow leftward out of the frame.
In the background, the apple leaves shine
      against the deep shade around the trunk.
In the foreground, my grandfather's hand, hangs down
      his lanky length—has been caught
just above its silhouette on the bare ground,

a dirt I know. The picture makes me feel found.
      My father's father's strong fingers—one set resting
on his only boy's thigh, the other open in the gesture
      of harvest, thumb slightly out, opposable, as if picking
a tomato or pole bean or pear—are in action, untouched
      by arthritis. My father's hands are for toys.
His face is my son's. His ears. The picture is a mirror
      I see into across seventy-two years,
a caught moment of the motion that made me,
      that made Micah and Graham in the image of us three.

I rest in the shade of those two acres,
the father who fed his family from them,
the father they grew. My own growth gathered itself there.
Day by day, secondhand sun is slowly taking back
this instant of light on apple leaves and these fathers.
No pain. It can't take back the fruit, the grain,
or the grip of the roots. It can't take back my name.

Last Week of Summer

My son stops cleaning out his backpack to bring me
in a baggie his last lost tooth, pulled at school,
a rust of blood where the root broke. The molar
seems to mock the Zip-Loc—no protection beats
its own substance, which seems eternal, the crown
a buff terrain made of twelve years of meals,
the first all milk. I thumb the sharp edge, round
and jagged, then turn it over—see the ivory apse,
intimate and vascular, cool snow-cave of infancy.
I think, as fathers do, how the root pushed through
the hot, teething gum, kept its grip against the sucking
of the thumb and the silly, muscular antics of the tongue –
how it knew, as few fathers do, to let go once the job was done.

His Empty Oil Tin

Small, round, its screw-on spout slender as a steeple,
  the tip crooks like Adam's finger on the Sistine ceiling
(or like God's. He was as old as God, as able and original,
  better at sparing his tools from wear). Use has dimmed
and burnished the bronze finish. My hand wants to take it up,
  old vessel suited to its use, to fit its curve between my first
and second fingers and let my thumb love the springy, instant
  return of its pressed base, the tree frog chirp it makes:
the crick of tending. This spout-tip touched bead after bead
  to axels, gears, bearings. It kept a house of quiet hinges.
He taught it to my father, this male care—the worth
  of easing friction, the clean, greasy smell, the worn shine.
  The oiled, silent song of the work going on.

The Morning After My Lecture on Cliché

As I drive the boys to school, sunrise unrolls its usual ecstasy
across the low edge of our local earth—the horizon
a seashell's inner cinnabar softened and unscrolled.
From our dim vinyl sanctum, we watch day open—
a steeple braises, then a cell tower, skeletal, blinking at its hips
and tip. Morning's offering reddens the altar of our dashboard.
Do I ask or does it, pentecostal, *Can I get a witness?*
Against this daily magma wash we go our daily way.
                              Oh, how bright the path
                              grows from day to day.
An old, fleeting newness wets this minute.
Nothing is repeated. Nothing is cliché.

Hummingbirders

The neighbor hangs one feeder only,
since '04—an hourglass he quakingly climbs
   a stepstool to hook to a chain in easy eye-
shot of his porch swing—and when this morning
   I see him see me as he stumbles going up,
it seems I ought to help, though our yard signs at election
   time have always kept our conversations brief.
We're both sure we know each other's mind.
   In the years of silence, his wife has greeted my kids
by name. We've loaned tools and sugar, been polite,
   almost kind. These needy, miniature buzz-bomb hummers
are a beauty we have in common. In their sip and zither,
   their sign-of-the-cross before the plastic blooms
our reverence aligns. How many summers can he feed the birds
   I watch for free? So I go up his steps. He holds the grail
of nectar out. We'll feed them together. I hang it,
   saying the kids love their green glitter and the thrum
of their flight. *Hell*, he says. *I just like to watch them fight.*

When Fears Try to Seize Me and Freeze Me Up

I reach in and unpocket my knife. To hold it closed
in my hand—its folded blade, punch, Phillips, file,

and saw, its weight and thrift of design—is to hope
that competence will come to me, as it has before:

some one of these tools will partner with my wits
and my wrist, my eye and thumb (so opposable, so

tuned to torque) to snug or free the set-screw that bleeds
a small, contingent engine, or cut to needed length

a hank of twine. She can nib a lead for writing, cut
a cane for fishing, or strip the wire that pipes music

or power through to do its work. The fresh, butter-white
slice of apple opened by her edge—ask my father,

my sons—has a sharper, sweeter meat, a tingle that
returns when I heft her, oiled and honed. Able. Neat.

To Put on Jeans Is to Pray

These Levi's I'm pulling on are letting go,
as denim so distinctively does—first the fade
   like the shifting colors overhead on a moody day,
then the imprint on the outside of my pockets
   of what they carry within—a rhombus of wallet
on my right rump, the shape of my jack knife
   rubbed into my right front, and, last, the wear
that threads the cuffs, knees, seat, and each thigh—
   and so am I. The night I bought them off a markdown
rack, I had eased away from my daughter and her mom
   trying on prom dresses: my opinion was one too many
and my presence made Emma emerge from the dressing
   room to be seen in all the uncertainty of her shopping
by everyone there. So I de-escalated down to menswear
   and found these, so blue they were black, with stretch,
suited to my short frame and shape, nothing like the stiff
   stovepipes my mother bought me in high school, which
I paired with my tux jacket for my own prom's after-parties.
   I liked the tension between the textures: my daily dungarees
versus this one-night-only Gatsby-me. The wry memory
   let me let go of feeling left out—landed me in the sixteen-year-
old's suspension of selves (son, brother, boyfriend, buddy)
   that had offered me too many shapes. It let me let her be.
I still see her smile in the cell pic she sent me—her pleased face
   (she fakes it well, but you can tell by her eyes), her light,
limber self like a white bud, the dress her deep blue vase.
   The last seven years I've worn these jeans have been
the one night she lived that gown, plus her daily blooming since.
   Thank you. Also, more please, of this threadbare, sky-blue grace.

Husbandry

My house, on the eve of any day I'm off, lets a crisis or raccoon creep
in. Seven long weekends running, a toilet has leaked, a light fixture
flickered; ants in a dry black seethe have blitzkrieged the pantry,
the sump pump has gone arrhythmic. All I can do is tend her needs.

At first, I raged. Now I've made a solace of the tool shed where,
over years, a kit has accrued—epoxies and voltage detectors and clear,
sweet poisons. Circuit testers and traps. A paper bag holds every form
of flapper valve. Two fixes have come so quick I've sat sipping
my reward longer than I labored. Most kept me hours on my belly

in a crawl space or an oven of an attic among live wires. The guys
at the hardware know me by my scent of crypt dust and sweat.
They help me like an adopted brother: *This'll get you from PVC to pex,*
they say. They know the last locksmith still cutting skeleton keys,
and which primer grips plastic. Where I swear at a seized-up gear,
they do triage— let it teach. They know every breakdown jerry-builds

a man. Learning when to wet-sponge gypsum mud, when to sand.
Finding out what'll lube a stuck lock, how to hook a butt of shoe mold
with a jackknife to fake a mitred corner. To flash a chimney, solder
copper pipe, glaze a pane—the exact heft of hammer-blow that will
reseat the dribbling shower stem – the thumbs and knuckles that have
done it all (file an edge onto the axe, feather plaster, and coping-saw
a curve into oak) seem an old, omniscient uncle's or a stranger's.

I listen for the creak, the drip, the draft, the breaker-box snap
with which she says *Let it begin.* Her 'coon beds in insulation,
smacks, rubs together his little criminal hands. Each time, I'm sure
the fixer won't show. Then home rebuilds me again.

Home Boys

I pry my eyes open at the end of strange dreams—
my fishing and writing friend, his cancer beat, sits
across a coffee shop table from me, listening,
then I'm alone in the sky, not flying, unable to fall,
high above a dim river that snakes into a bay—

and rise, pull on jeans, fry an egg taco for my son,
sixteen, who says he needs to dress '50s for extra credit.
I give him a white t-shirt, roll up his dungarees
above his snowy socks and loafers. He wants my old, gold
letterman's jacket. As he shrugs it on, the radio reports

Evans, Georgia is the best place in the nation to live.
I was his age, in the McDonald's there, when two rednecks
in line behind me saw the letter jacket's black T and hissed
We'll kick your Thomson ass just as Stoney and Royce
came out of the men's room. *Quit talking about my friend's ass,*

Stone-bone said. They did. Best fries and Coke I ever had.
I savor the fizz and salt as I hand Graham his lunch, then watch
from the porch as his Hyundai rolls off into the dawn,
my middle-aged Thomson ass not flying, not falling, not alone.

Dearth of the Cool 2017

Four decades of punching above my hipster weight
had done my chill detachment in. No one notices even
    the earliest adopter once he's as old as a velociraptor.
Either the alt-culture's current had ramped up to a blur
    or got slacker and slacker—I couldn't tell for sure.
Lots of the hyped things I'd been first to find now felt like lore–
    Red Stripe, flanged guitar, Let's Active, DMs from
thrift stores. *Sick throwback* a skate punk said in '07 of a cap I bought
    new in '92. Even then I'd footnote to death an ecstatic jam,
lionizing or ironicizing a one-second sample of Miles or McTell.
    By my mid-40s, my go-to gab partners at def parties were
peeling away at my approach. I started stopping myself pre-spiel.
    The gall of being blackballed from the prescient remnant
grayed my goatee. 43 was Bizarro 13—younger kids, not older had
    the street cred. Not just invisible or uncool, man. Dead.

    Word: one Wednesday in Wax N Facts
an ex-roadie—he's eighty if he is a day—in a CBGB T turns from
    the dollar bin he's mining to offer me a CD. *'Member Lou?*
The Dinosaur Jr. dude? Here's his trip-hop band.
    I take it with a shrug. Folk Implosion: a buck. I humor
the old fart. I put it in as I drive home in the dark. I play it daily
    'til I hit 50. For every one of those spins, I pine to thank him
for these tracks I could still not-know, stranger who didn't get me
    my bogus groove back, but laid me a real one. Age-Nazi me
recalls his pewter ponytail and the flake and fade of OMFUG, but
    not his face. He's in the actual Home of Underground Rock
by now—like all saints, uber uncool—and so, to that elder bro
    of Moreland Ave, martyred by yours untruly, I say: *You rule*
and pour out the forty (actually a twelve of microbrew).
    Intercede, please, for depthless wannabe dipshits like me,

we the o-so-righteous. Help us to seek and find and hand out free
the funk, the b-side beauties. Give us your higher fidelity.

After Tom's Father Died

Two weeks after the graveside,
Tom brings to my front porch a box:
antique tins of split-shot sinkers,
weedless hooks in clear zip bags
turning brittle, a Bomber Bushwhacker
that has at least ten years on me,
on ambush in its ambered box.

If any one of these hits the water, Tom says,
 that's better than throwing it away.
We've paddled all of two rivers together,
not fast, just too brisk for me to fish
(though on the Flint four years ago
I landed three bass on four casts
when we beached to pee).

My dad wasn't much for fishing.
The Bushwhacker eyes me with
its ebony pupil, barbs out, red along
its back, gold-orange glitter on its flank.
Its maw gapes around the eyelet—bellicose.
The lure poses less as prey than provocation,
with a vintage ingenuity, tooled and wise

to a largemouth's aggression, bronze barbs
as brutal as the colors are beautiful -- lifelike,
like life, which, the old folks used to say,
is a casting off. Because I was eleven and lived
for June evenings hooking bedding bluegill
from farm ponds, I heard *Life is a casting out—*
fishing meant catching. All I had to do was go.

As soon as possible, I'll tie the Bomber on
and toss it into a tangle of tree roots in the edge
of the Ocmulgee. I'll treasure it by risking its loss.
To feel it shudder through the current is a way
to honor my friend's father. Together, casting off,
casting out, we may land a lunker on that living water.

My Father Falls Asleep Holding a Cup of Black Coffee

He sits upright on the couch, his eighty-fifth Christmas
unswaddled around him, the chatter of grandchildren
not quite enough to keep him with us. His full cup stays

level and steady, though his eyes are closed. Only asleep
can he look so grave, his lips and eyelids almost clenched,
as if in big decision, his back straighter than when he's awake.

When I try to take the mug—not one drop has he spilled
or sloshed—the strength in his fingers startles me. So does
the depth of his rest, unruffled by my shuffle and rustle

through the wreckage of giftwrap, or by my firm pull
on the cool joe. I recall his palming of slow-pitch softballs,
his gapping of the plugs we've snugged into his trucks. His knots.

His cup hand is his chord hand that walks the bass down the frets
of his Martin on Wildwood Flower. Winter nights in his greenhouse
the same left fingers cupped a clot of Big Boy seedlings for the right's

thumb and pointer to pinch and transplant one by one into flat
after flat of soil he mixed himself. Just as I appreciate his hold,
he lets go, suddenly. A drop slips down the mug, but I recover,

using the touch he taught me, that lures a bass by twitching the line,
knows ripe corn from green, lefty-looses/righty-tights.
His hand is my own, stronger. I wonder if a son ever feels grown.

Slough

As my dawn run brings me to a bridge in the woods,
I glimpse myself flash across a pool of leaf-
flecked sky and I hear my father's voice say,

forty years ago, *slough*, meaning this sort of mirror—
a still remainder of rain in the forest floor.
At twelve, I heard *slew*—as in *many, a lot*:

a slew of relatives crowding our house, a slew
of trouble. Also, what Bard's black arrow did
to Smaug. I heard the verb as a sword-slash

cleaving a head clean off. He meant the mini-pond
he then took me to, where his deft right wrist cast
a green spring lizard into a flooded gully of clouds

like the one I'm passing over. The lure shattered
the sky, then descended into treetops filled
with bluegill and small bass. As the water healed,

the other father in it wobbled and resolved, a quiet
knower of names, a shade. The line slit sideways
through this shadow. He set the hook, then handed me

the rod. I landed the fish—dragged him thrashing
from the sky. Grounded and heaving, he hated me
with his dragon eye. We let him go. Kept his pride.

I cross the bridge in three strides, reeling in a last mile.
The words, the undrowned forest floor, my father's fish
and mine, they float me. For three steps, I'm light as a child.

Letter to My Brother from the Seven Islands Shoals

Running the river alone to get away, to wordlessly
      pray, I match the current blurring between boulders.
            It carries me and holds me in place. I have saddled
               a snake that journeys through forms—
that hisses and chops through rocks, then, soundless, glisses
      'round a bend. Under me, the muscle of dew, rain,
            second-hand sea, underground aquifer, ripples.
      If I could stay writ on this rolling liquid
I would be delivered like a letter to its delta
      that never wrote to me. Your poems carry me down
            each shoal, my boat's bow blunt as your worn pencil,
               busy as your bluetick's snout tracking 'coon.
Nosing through the rapids, I ride your gurney
      through the hospital hall. That glide is this one.
            Your pen trickled postcard poems from your chemo
chair that bear me along. Sent mail, like this boat's bottom,
      takes damage getting there. What that travels doesn't?
The Ocmulgee scars itself: sandbars sift downstream,
      soil sucks from under sycamores, island points strain
            planks, trash, and whole trees into drifts of accidental
architecture. This is to show you these isles, how they lean
      upstream, resisting the flow. Their trees' branches
            so nearly span the channel—so nearly touch the bank's
               boughs—that they make a living cave,
      a corridor of breath, a green gullet as apt to cradle
as to swallow sticks, skiffs, whatever comes.
      The river can't help it. It has to go—snow to stone to

stream, culvert to creekbed, journey
        between oceans that weaves from well to well,
          breathed into then out of thunderheads.
      If in this long loop, this huge pouring zero,
   feeding and breaking the mountains' bones,
 one of us slips under—so?

Where either of us goes, the other will follow.

Who can straighten what he has made crooked?

—Ecclesiastes 7:13

The real question is who would want to—
　　　curve of my wife's cheek and lower spine
curl of fiddlehead and of my son's forelock
　　　kinked strength of willow walking stick
my brother sawed free from a knuckly web
　　　of bent roots to give to me its heartwood squiggle—
who to all of these crunknesses
　　　just as they are
would not say yes?
　　　To everwhose hands grip each growing life (one
at beginning, one at end)—then bend
　　　　　　　　　　　　I try to open my own.

The Boy's First Breast

(other than his mother's, of course)
he didn't see, but more richly sensed
as his cousin pressed him to her
in a birthday half-hug—the yielding
swell, the give of her from beyond
girlhood, from a bend rounded,
a sudden place of perfect bloom.
Her person was a kept promise of
softness. This tender assertion
in passing placed him—made him
feel like a buried root mining the loam
for the sake of a high white blossom.
His whole body gathers around
where hers so briefly meets him.
He is only grazed by the ordinary
give and resist of growth, yet
she opens in him for all his life
the grown son's ache. She lets go.
Smiles. The candles melt on his cake.

Found Boot

floated sole-up down the Blackwater
'til it eddied under Rae's high rock
for a day and night for her to climb

down with her book and find and know the nails
in the heel to be her cobbler uncle's. Rae poled
it out and took it to town: some man was dead.

A one-eyed dog roamed the river road all week,
slower and slower, the drowned man's feist,
scared, skinny as the squirrels he no longer treed.

Rae put on the boot: he came to her,
doubtful, doleful, wolfed a moldy biscuit.
Tauble the dead man, dog master: cobbler's bill.

So Rae named the dog to honor the drowner
and let him sleep with the boot 'til soon he calmed.
On the high rock she played him little songs

on her Hohner. Each day, dark came earlier.
Rae and Taub both felt found. The other boot
was winched up that spring from a well in town.

The Clay County Stringer: Horses Struck by Lightning

The owner won't talk or let me shoot the scorched tree—
maybe he hates the paper, maybe he grieves.
The neighbor, Kay, used her backhoe to bury them.
She assumes my interest is as tender as hers—
four horses and a foal. She remembers no thunder.

It's not pity, not wonder, just the job—my editor
makes me ask. Farms need news, not features.
They'll work afraid if they trust their rider, the neighbor says.
They's loyal creatures. The vet wants charges pressed.
Any animal goes to that oak in the rain. A good husband

saves his stock from itself. Damned shame. A gelding,
a pinto, two mares. The foal lived an hour. No open flame,
just a vertical char-mark, crown to ground. From her barn loft,
Kay points out to me the tree, four acres off. The one horse
I've known by name (I really liked the girl who groomed him)

was hard to look in the eye, easy to admire. Every place
you stroked that horse was hard. That's not news rural readers
can use, but the way she brushed him (Delonair) was. She would
have let me, but it was him she loved. He knew it. You could
see it in either one of his eyes. My lede will be *The oak survived.*

Hound Farmer's Funeral

His slow nephew, Lile, was likely the one let them out
      to run baying and whining into the dirt lot
            outside the church. Inside, folks tried to look out,
but the glass just gave back Jesus, Noah, and Job in
      the same old poses, turned almost new
            by the barking behind them, that true witness,
drowning the hymn in howls and *bwooos*,
      the animal throats calling lost and found at once.
            The feist's gut-bay from creek-bottom briers,
from laurel hells past midnight and clefts of rock,
      now raised for the hand that fed, for the horned latch finger
            and its fellows that set down the bowl of meat,
for the two-leg voice and the metal smell that drug them from dell
      and holler, voice that came into darkness and belly-wetting
            slough, the old call far and dim then coming, coming,
growing under the ears as coon spoor does in the nose and tooth,
      until it was there, a must, strong as his hand.
      Even the lead dog had to heed.
In the red clay lot they hunt the voice that found them.
      Blueticks and brindles moil and forepaw the muddy fenders
            of his truck, now another's, as if to tree the owner.
The oak door opens: a scent under iris, lilac, and the sick-sweet
      balm of the dead like a green gas points them and raises
            the boss dog's hackles. Year-olds belly-down. Cower.
The long box comes down the two plank steps among them:
      each hound is his own whirl in the boiling eddy of the pack,
           all sounding at once, surrounding him.
When the hearse door shuts, they hush.

After He Flags a Bus Outside Okmulgee, Oklahoma

he draws eyes, then the brows above them rise to the snaps
on his shirt—so bright they make a scene in the morning sun.

What man boards a bus studded with mother of pearl?
No one snorts out loud as they all turn away—except

a pre-ex-wife, 44, in the back, resigned to riding a second day
to her mother's in Phoenix, which is not far enough away.

She stares at the luster of the studs. Cowboy shirts, her brother
Tim called them. He would grab each half of his, just below

the collar, and yank it open neck to tail. She hears it yet,
that freeing volley of pops that pleased him so. Right off

he'd snap them shut again, starting at the hem. Thanks
to Tim, there is this one male jewelry that agrees with her.

She will watch after he sits across the aisle from her, when,
forty miles in, he'll unclick his denim cuffs to turn back

his sleeves. The russet hair on his forearm will all flow
one way, like river grass under a clear current—a gliss

that will carry her into an Arizona pawn shop to hock
her ring, make a new start. She will buy a white dress

with white snaps only she can press together or tug apart.

Sub

That one day substitute teaching did him in,
made him into a substitute self: he read out loud
to his seventh-grade scientists *We are mostly water*
and became a mizzling rain right there in the classroom,
coming down soundlessly and evaporating, not even running off,
not dripping into pools, not collecting. He was all cloud inside
his tweed jacket and tie, an overdressed mist, his substance gone,
the far-off ocean calling him down creeks and culverts and through
layers of limestone to its uneasy body. The children didn't notice.
They seemed watery, too—narrow but deep, like wells.
They weren't going anywhere. He was. He was only a sip,
a faint fog with no nourishment to offer, no force of flood,
no volume to dissolve any solid. What was there to say?
He fell silent. Quiet settled on the down of their arms.
Soon thy would hear it and one by one look up
from the book and find themselves alone
under an air laced with dew.

Poem on a Prine Lyric

Ain't it funny how an old broken bottle
looks just like a diamond ring?
                    —John Prine

Shirl, sixteen, wants the stone because it's an accident
that's nobody's fault, a clear rock crunk from the shift
of continents, a seed pearl squeezed from earth's
hot bed. The early, oldest mating, mantel on crust,
eked this bitty chip of glitter, and so to loop one
from your lover is to zero down deep, to tap the tectonic:
She'll say *I plight thee my troth* and make geology wobble.
Daddy ought to ask her: *You want all this on one finger?*
Think of mountains worn to nubs, cliffs calving into oceans.
The world'll grind you harder where you're going
than it has where you've been. Daddy won't. Too late to,
considering the things she's already done done.
He thinks of her at twelve, aiming at bottles with his .410—
mad when she missed, crowing when she blew one into gems.

III. Leaving No Trace

Note at the Trailhead

Habituated bears have cut
bear bag lines tied too low.

Let this be a sign unto you, I go, as we walk
into the mountain's maw, slowed by heavy packs.
We're snacks carrying snacks. Good to know.
Grimey gives a little fake laugh: *Tie it high—*
so? A cub with a K-bar can still climb.
Do they chew the cord? Click out
one claw and saw through? We
drop the subject once we begin
to descend down into the noun
both our brains
are verbing:
gorge.

Trail

Between firs, among aspens, stone to stone across
a white creek, through furzy tussocks of meadow
sogged with thaw, up gritty pitches by steep switch-
backs of scree to a high slope of summer snowfield
winds this ribbon of wear—a scar making a *here*
by flowing to a *there*. Take care to keep on it,
though your boots dig it deeper, though for whole miles
you hump a ditch. Dry air will carry off a breath
of dust each step: rock sifted to soil, thin as silt—
a wear you wear, a ground-smoke to drift over a drop-off
or foot-log. Grizzly, ankle-breaking hole, slab-teeter,
coral snake, storm—these killers the trail abides, in the lee
of boulders, over the pass, as it leads you beside still waters,
lays you in a valley of shadow, as it takes you in stride.

Black Kettle Grasslands, Oklahoma

The August stars vanish. The night comes
still and sweats. When the prairie's distant edge
flickers, I sweep the halo of my headlamp
over the ground: rucked, lumpy, aerated
by anthills, damp nearer the small lake.
I pitch at last a minute before midnight
under two trees on a slight, level rise.
My stakes lost, I sharpen sticks to pin
my corners, cross the poles and arc them,
clip on the cloth, cast over it all the fly
like a surf net and cinch it down. My pack
wrapped, I zip in—lie sweating on my pad
in this slight shelter, floating each slow minute
closer to the sound of a river shoal, along
the marshy edge of sleep. A curtain of air
cold as a ghost drops on me, chilling the salt
on my skin. The right wall of nylon bulges in,
out, in. Rain's paw-pads rake the roof, thunder
crumples, and all that's outside my sheath flares
once, then sizzles. The sternum-crack of a mortar shell
detonates directly over my bed, lightning quickening
until it strobes. My capsized skin boat quakes
and shudders, straining against the swells. I keep
still inside her, chilled, certain she will founder,
accepting. Two drops tap my thigh, marking me
for some gale-dug grave. I give myself up
to the rip and the wave, to the branch
that will brain me—then open my eyes
in a rinsed yellow morning. She unzips,
water breaking from the fly: I crown
into the bright wide open, crawl beached
and blinking out to glimpse the horizon

going on without me, the soggy, sunlit scar
of the trail. I turn and bow in thanks to my taut,
whole veil, stretched over two strung bows,
bent and strong—her shape is the D in *dwell*.

Cheat River: Packing the Pack

We gather together to ask the gorge's blessing
armysocks in nylon shorts in old shirt in pack towel
in wool sweater, freeze-dried food book-flat in foil
pouches, a can of beans, two cups in two bowls in cook
pot, thin tent rolled tight, and sleeping bag
all nested in the pack, wound 'round by my therm-a-rest,
as placental of my gear as it will be under me.

Next, zipped in baggies:
raincoat and cap,
poems, coffee, creamer, wipes,
duct tape, compass, AAs, AAAs, headlamp, binocs,
notebook, spork, Bic, pen, cord, torch, patches, soap.

In side pockets: water, jug and jug.

See, Shaver's Fork of the Cheat, our thrift, our perfectly poor kit?
In voluntary poverty we come to honor your excesses, your prodigal
pissing away of current and scree, birch, fir, and teasel, your miles
of sky left lying for every passing thief. Spent sandstone and chert,
blown vaults of turned and polished pebbles — we pack light
to promise your shredding of feral tender will not be wasted on us.

Truck stuck by gully-rut in the logging road, we carry in what will
carry us through, down dissolving mountain trail nettle-edged,
boot squelch in a bog patch. Rockcrop tripspot about drops Bill,
then{though I go softshoe}me until we lay our minimal all
in the crisp flame of your meadow grass and fish.

We give back the first green-black bass as soon as you grant her,
writhing, outraged in clear air. Each one hooks me like a live wire
grabbed: plunge of hunger, thrum of muscle fed. The dead quicken

in the packed feathers of flesh that fights me, death the life in you,
Cheat, the current in you, each fish a current in your current.
Your bass who catch us we release. Hip-deep in your unscrolling,
lit wicks of cold, we throw ourselves back, (not) standing still
in the current, (not) real. We two not two, mountain and river (not)
two. Shysters' drop and flash our widow's mite, our offering.

Emptied, we come in gloam to what we packed in.
We unroll, see what we can live without. We lean into the lack.
Bill cracks branches. I pitch the skin we will sleep in.

Smallmouth retell their stories.
We let the fire lick our wounds.

Two stars

Four

Our beans begin to bubble.

High Falls, Shaver's Fork of the Cheat River, Late June

Because we have backpacked from Bemis
between the gleam of the tracks, boots on gravel
all the way, I'm done in by every suppleness I witness:
current rounding over a river-wide warp of stone,
drift sticks licked gray and skinless by the pour
until they're vascular and tenderized, vulnerable
as the inside of a girl's wrist, the rhododendron thicket's
springs and bends and green slap fight of passage that musks
me up with semi-stiff rubbings. Branches bow, neither
low nor high, but always—always—mid-thigh.
                              Still, I pass
upstream, descend again down the moss boing of bank
to the clear bustle of a deep hole below a shoal.
The surface is a warble of cold through which brook trout,
fearless, see me magnified, their fins fingering the cobbled bottom.
God, the give and resistance of this old, broken whole, the flow—
the easy hold of each fish in the Cheat's ceaseless blow. I'll not fool
one, but the river has me, too—rod, soul, mind. So I throw and throw
and throw.
              Daylight runs out. The bright rails and black ties, wave
and laurel and brook and hole—they all go. Mountain and river roll
into a single shadow, still not speaking, in words I ought to know.

Brown's Mount, November Noon

I've been told
     the spiders that web off the path to the high,
piney knoll have *book lungs*. The band of wild pigs
I hear traipsing through down-slope are a *drift* or a *drove*
(hogs would make a *passel*): to take these names on faith
seems easy here, alone, where the stride of the day, neither
quick nor slow, flips old leaves in autumn solitaire and *now*
lasts long enough to browse the library of orb-weaver breath.
Do book lungs close and open on a spine, perfect-bound?

    On this rock ridge, the drift of me will calm and settle,
each page of me be breeze- and daylight-turned -- caressed,
not read. Like the lichen, I'm here to breathe, not learn. Still,
my brain flips through the passel of things I should become.
I tell my mind to let me, like spiders, pines, and this rise
of fossil coral, just be: *Hello, cosmos? This is your frontal lobe,*
calling to book its lobotomy.

    that would leave no wild son to thumb from the seashells
in this boulder a new Braille for *beautiful*. Each pig
in the drove, every argiope's constellation of spiracles and cliff-
stone needs a witness, a heart-mind that beats on by draw-
ing in these breaths, that collects page by page what can't
and must be read and binds it all into one body, spine, soul—
one book of active rest.

Otter Letter

This is just to rave about the wave you are
on the 'Hootch's waves, until you dive slick
as a round silk rope rolling over an oiled pulley.
Your fingered hind feet emerge, kicking, before
your tail (serif then sans) and all your afterparts
follow your geezer-face down to whisker the bottom.
When you surface on your back, smacking
as you gnaw crawdad off the plate of your chest,
native grace drowns out your bad manners.
What ripples the river ripples you, noodle spine,
eel of mammals. How can you be both coiled
and slack—simultaneously hyper and lax?
Your swim is Chinese dragon flight, your bound
up the bank a wet, fluid script (brush not pen) of a rollicking,
self-singing hymn that dissolves when you limbo back in.
Now you're gone, the river seems sad, the banks blank. Forgive
my cursive, clunkier than you—but I couldn't not say thanks.

Passage

Some of these logs wants to be canoes.
　　　　　　　　　　　　　—Tony Johnson

Mornings when I wonder whether I have survived,
　　when I wake up sure that the bubble of my soul
has burst, leaving a soapy slick of phantom pain
　　　　　inside this body that goes right on eating, breathing
　　and breaking up storm sticks for the rusting fire pit,
I think of the canoes of the Clatsop—not the ones
　　　　　coveted and eventually stolen by Lewis and Clark
　　because they were deft and *neet* and never flipped
in the feral chop of the Columbia, across which
　　　　　they carried the first horses to come to that country—
　　but the one crafted nine generations later, when
a carver from the Quinault people came, found a cedar
　　　　　eight centuries old fallen in the Cascades ten years before
　　and brought the Clatsop and Nehalem to it with fire, boiling
water, adzes, wedges, and axes, to let the high grove's loss
　　　　　help them remember and render again an old shape
　　that might ship more seawater than Coboway Tyree's
least boat, but that still would prow the Pacific and bear
　　　　　six men out into a chaos of brine and back to the stones
　　of the beaches they belong to, as this dream of strangers,
singing the spirit into white cedar, bears me to mine.

Ocmulgee Drought

Drought has drawn the river clear
                             down to its deepest crease.
My boat follows the flow under the flow,
               this rainless summer having winnowed
      the swollen, bank-to-bank python-seethe
                 of May to a single feral sinew I can see
                     the grainy bottom through –
light brown sugar on the inside of bends,
                         rapt sandstone on the out.

All day long I cruise an inch above grounding
                   on the hiss of this wide rill. Open mussels,
       flaking mica,
    and beer cans from decade before last blasted bare silver
flash from their other world.
                The rapture cometh soon. The depth that hides lives,
             shells, a mud-grip tire, silt-filled bottles,
   has burned down to this last current -- a low, fiery wind I ride
                   over an ochre desert.

      Minnows, a water spider, then an elver eel (*s*-ing) glide
alongside me for an instant each. So little is enough to hold us all
           up and hand us along. They twitch and go, not seen,
                still there, remnant pilgrims in a remnant flow
                    that will pour us into the Forks,
                       the Altamaha, the ocean
                           in one winding, trans-
                             parent, undying

                      motion.

This Handful of Clay, Wise Creek

says my next body will be accrued of other bodies
a remnant slurry that rain will gather to the river
to be carried to where a bend catches us and

layers us into a lens. Will we be a congregation?
A confluence? Will each mote of me within
the wash of others whisper, cackle, or curse

according to its loves, aches, and losses—
will we make a din like the shattered chitter
of a shoal? No answer. Clay has a way of

coming quiet at last—alluvial and still Current
slowing lays it down in lines, a legible geology
composed by decomposing. Not a choir on risers,

but their song, minus parts and rounds, a low, simple
unison of animal loam. A slippery, wordless hymn,
without sound. Just the breathing of the ground.

Estuary

Strangers here—all people are in marshes—we can't tell
    whether it fills or empties.
                The spartina greens on pluff and salt,
its own mazey acre of prosperity—a wealth
                    of filth and death, a lowlife of slick,
glissando silt where river and sea meet
       to settle up and launder their reeking gains.
This heavy brine is an ebb
             of everything alive enough to die—
    even the tide. The mud prickles with inky crabs.
        We hear them writing lies.

Ripple

The wimple of water on Sapelo's beach—
the wrinkle in the Altamaha's bend widening
from the mullet's jump—the *O*s where
the flat rock skipped in three quick kisses
of Falling Creek crossing to the other side—

the wavering shadow the noon sun scrawls
as it shoots through Ocmulgee shallows
onto sandstone the shade of a wave,
a silty, solar cursive having its delible say—

the opening outward, in ring after ring
of pain, of the womb's amniotic sea until
its bed breaks: a mother comes to be—

the warble through water, light, and blood
of the one circle that each life briefly centers,

rippling from, rippling to, before it seems to cease—

IV. Weather to Make Yourself

Being a poet is a condition.
—Robert Frost

Some Suns

There's really only one, I know:
the long, lone, slo-mo exploding
that makes the solar system go.
Still, frames of it seem so singular –
the day my teenage dungarees dried
on the line in 99 degrees, the straight-legs
of the Levis baked so stiff they ironed smooth
my prune-y, post-swim skin. I felt like a snake,
warmed from the outside in.

Also, the afternoon it gemmed every drop of rain
in a mountain shower, making the air over the creek a stipple
of descending glitter and paying back the chill of my sopped shirt
and socks. A year later, my toddler son, strapped hours
in his car seat, crowed at the same sort of light
as we vanned through a barrage of
soybean-sprinkler spray. Dry inside that
one-second waterfall,
the family floated on his ripple of giggles.

On Orrest Head in the late '80s, a day as gray
and still as lead leaked a single starved shaft
of sunset onto a sudden hare bedded in bracken. It lit
the red thread of his pulse through his ears. I listen to him listen.

Call me a cheery nitwit to cherry-pick and particle-ize Sol's
steady stream, which also haloes murders and melts ice
from under Arctic bears -- but I can't stay salty
recalling the bright dream my wife woke me to in '95, when we owed
on everything: the power out, the bedroom windows lit by snow.
Like that wedding-cake white, I can't not reflect that moment
of sun. I have to hand along that plain, free,
one and only light.

Weather to Make Yourself

Do I sit and soak in Wilco's growl of guitar,
      waiting for words to emerge from the reverb
or do I chip a sentence from the block of silence
      that sits on my desk, just shy of snapping its legs?
On the cracked plain of wood there's my notebook
      and a polar bear, caught mid-stride by François Pompon—
a Christmas-ornament copy of the enormous original
      in the d'Orsay. He is the snowy lope of motion, of winter,
and of the will under all animal wanderings. *What I do*
      is me, Hopkins's kingfisher cries, *For that I came*—
lines I love, a way I'd like to be, but too psalm-y
      for my bear's huge, mute paws, his soft, lethal gravity.
His entire mass exists in motion. Even his sleep is a flow.
      I know this by Pompon's subtraction: he carved in every
characteristic, then, draft by draft, let details go until he saw
      essence—the least that had to be there to realize bearness—
then sang it in stone. Ur *ursus*, nothing extra. Here I sit,
      in the marble's full silence, "Muzzle of Bees" helping me hear
whether I myself am/have/risk/*essai* a word-bear to make live bears
      more real—an art that keeps by learning what to take away.

Even the dirt

kept breathing a small breath, says Ted Roethke
in his bit about the root cellar. I carry that lungful
myself—the dirt more than the breath, the damp dust
ague of my grandmother's earth-walled room
of shelved preserves, the jars creepily lit by the one bulb,
crude oil jewels collecting their sift of grit from the floor above.
We've met, Ted, only in your poems and in your teaching
of my teacher's teachers, yet you can say how loam unmakes me—
how that rectangular, house-roofed grave grew me.

My father made soil. Bales of peat moss, foot-tubs of perlite,
vermiculite, and sweet yellow sand that I mixed with a hoe
for him to sprout seeds in. You should smell it wet, that Milky Way
of muck. A soaked flat glittered like a candle in a mica mine.
There's no counting the neighbors and strangers who ate what it grew,
the fruit it breathed out from burial, as dirt will always do.

Cutting Back Brush

Cutting back brush at our lot's wild edge in late April,
I seized a locust sapling that stabbed through a thick glove
into my palm where the spine-tip broke off inside me.
My own fist did it—my own muscle closing on the thorn,
then recoiling as the pain pierced my left hand, which crawled
mid-air like a spider pinned in a bug collector's box. My trying
to let go drew the curved black barb too deep into my meat to see.
Keen as the sting was, I didn't bleed. For eight weeks, to grip
anything with that weaker hand—soup pot, ball mit, bike handlebar,
hardback book, even the bare hip of my lover—hurt like a deep bone
had bruised. My bilateral body turned mono in the way it moved:
my right side kindly took on every small task to let the left heal,
but that opposable brother's answer was to soften and throb harder.
To touch my son's shoulder, steer my truck, and braid fingers
with my wife at a wedding dance drove a glass needle into a nerve.
I winced to even swim. The kid in my core who hid his splinters
from his father's hot tweezers, the digging point of his knife, knows
how a secret ache gradually grows visible. I didn't look as the thorn
slowly rose, a faint, penciled comma one shade darker day by day
until, this morning, wincing as I cupped the water to wet my face,
my pain is written in pen. I read it like a dash on the under
side of this page or the black back of a minnow that rides a spring
to its surface. With a straight pin, I spear through the ripple of skin.
Blood wells from the wound: the healing begins.

Bi-

Bi- as in *-ped*, as in *-cycle*—is the phoneme for me
in motion, the twoness of my legs loping a trail

or the sidewalk to work, the twin-spin of spoked
wheels rolling me out and back home with enough speed

to make a breeze, even uphill. My Fuji has twice
the axels of the entire inhabited solar system,

oh so oiled that they carry me like a king.
Every circle can be surfed if you wedge in

where the curl begins. What this means
for my bicameral brain, for my two-room heart,

my matched lungs, kidneys, and cajones
I can't precisely say, except that these twins make me

improvise always—keep me keeping my balance
between two whirling wholes that halve me. Body

and soul. Father and gland. Opposing poles
divide my home against itself and make it stand.

Eyes

Eyes, you used to seize every edge—
each stitch on a breaking baseball,

the inky undulation of Sister Sledge
as the LP grooved us back to the animal.

You tightroped the seams of cocktail dresses,
fell from the upended horizons of their hems.

The least ripple of a bedding bluegill's fin
across lit creek-bottom zeroed you in.

You were happy, Lefty, to shut as your bro
notched a Coors can's *o* then put a bullet through it—

but now, leaf blurs into bough, the sunflower petal
and the lamp flame melt into the same yolk-stroke

of Van Gogh. Reading is like tracking mice on snow.
So I'm writing it big: you're benched, bros.

Fingers, skin, you're in. Feel it all. Fill us. Know.

Hands

On demand they remember the chord, the half-hitch,
how to dig postholes after years of holding pencils,
the planting of long-fallow acres once they are fenced—
how to open loam, part roots, and drizzle seed.
   On instinct mine gather wild blackberries, then net birds
in the reaped thicket, though freeing a caught redwing
calls for conscious, tender muscle: a hold that grips with no
crushing, that weighs the give of down and hollow bones
and that thumbs softly the strobing chokecherry of the heart.
   Some hands see and hear, some are skilled in yielding—
can cup skim-ice, or a tea bowl webbed with cracks,
and the most lightly breakable bodies, intact. (One test
is to carry a dandelion, complete, rock to rock across a creek.)
   I knew a girl with palms and fingers so cool and limber
that salamanders cradled there sang. Hummers tried to, too.
Her touch tuned the frail, feather-light lacework of their lungs.
   Their senses and skills scare most of us, so, when we sleep,
we send our hands away, do things in our dreams without them.
They don't care. They are still there, married to their opposite
(who else?) and bearing it. *Just try to let us go*, they say. *Try.*

Ars Poetica

These gloves fit too big around your fingers,
      but the work they let you do is a man's:
lift the rotting, ground-bound log,
      seize and slash the wild rose canes
and the red-barbed blackberry. Wear
      them to grip and handle found bones
and the head-shot racoon that acted rabid.
      They're a tool of touch that shelters the body,
a back-pocket bravery to pull out and put on,
      a reverent use for the skins of the dead
(the only work doe-hide still does,
      padding the brush-hook's handle).
Long wear—unloading block trucks,
      punching post holes into the frozen farm,
hoeing nut grass from long rows of okra—
      leads to a bent love between them
and the fingers, so that, pulled off at dark,
      they are haunted by what they have held
and hauled. Even empty, lit under the barn's
      yellow, gnat-spattered bulb, they still sign
their strange work, so that, weary, washing
      for supper, a man sees their empty grasp
         as cold well water fills the cup of his hands.

Household God

There's an ear there, as you make the bed,
that will hear what you can't say—an eye
that reads the sign language of your hand

tucking the quilt, plumping from the pillow
the shape of a beloved sleeper's head.
When you pinch a bloom off an impatiens

in the hope of another blossom, some small
angel hearkens to the gratitude, however brief.
The deity watches the washing of the dog,

savors the cold, clean incense of sudsy fur,
then the hymn of him shaking dry and rolling
in grass, joyous to ruin your work. The almighty

asks to lie beside you under the warm Ford, watching
the black pour of fortyweight oil that has anointed
your wife's comings and goings and delivered

your daughter to school. The god of plunger-ing
the clog, of washing windows and priming the sump
and packing the lunch, the I AM of sorting spice jars

and ironing. The ping of each pea shelled into this pan
is a rosary bead, a ritual with no words—a grace of work,
a psalm-sound. You think you are the giver, the owner:

then you hear the only life there is, listening to you listen.
Both you and God feel found. There is only holy ground.

The Author

Gordon Johnston, award-winning author of *Seven Islands of the Ocmulgee*, *Scaring the Bears*, and *Durable Goods*, is co-author, with Matthew Jennings, of *Ocmulgee National Monument: A Brief Guide with Field Notes*. A former journalist, he teaches writing and literature at Mercer University.